SUNDANCE
AT DUSK

Al Purdy
SUNDANCE AT DUSK

McCLELLAND AND STEWART

Copyright © 1976 by Al Purdy

ISBN: 0-7710-7206-6

The Canadian Publishers
McClelland and Stewart Limited
25 Hollinger Road, Toronto

Printed and bound in Canada

For Jacko Onalik and Martin Senigak

BOOKS BY AL PURDY

The Enchanted Echo (1944)
Pressed on Sand (1955)
Emu, Remember! (1956)
The Crafte So Longe to Lerne (1959)
Poems for All the Annettes (1962)
The Blur in Between (1963)
The Cariboo Horses (1965)
North of Summer (1967)
Wild Grape Wine (1968)
The New Romans – Editor (1968)
Fifteen Winds (1969)
The Quest for Ouzo (1970)
Storm Warning – Editor (1970)
Love in a Burning Building (1970)
Selected Poems (1972)
Sex and Death (1973)
In Search of Owen Roblin (1974)
The Poems of Al Purdy (1976)
Storm Warning 2 – Editor (1976)

CONTENTS

SUNDANCE
AT DUSK

LAMENT

They are gone the mighty men
they have vanished utterly gone the record-setters
once as a child I remember
the achievers of forty feet at a brass spittoon
—and it sang like the birds

Uncle Wilfred was my non-uncle
I called him that because I loved him
sitting in the semi-darkness he could knock a fly
off the dinner dishes with one bronze splash
—my Uncle Wilfred will never die

Teamsters were lords of that kingdom
they raced their wagons and fought duels
they let go at open windows they had jumpy wives
nervous with close calls from straw-coloured fluid
an evil the preacher mentioned on Sundays

The Gilbert House had leather chairs in the lobby
and maybe half a dozen very old men
dozed there taking pot shots at the rubber tree
which died slowly and dust settled on them slowly
until Spang went the spittoon singing you're dead

When I lay in the grass staring at clouds
I imagined them up there sighting at planets
now the shoe-spattered targets and dead shot dowsers
blacksmiths horses teamsters all are gone—even at length
mouth pursed and ready my Uncle Wilfred

SUNDANCE

They travelled north from high plateaus
between the Sierra Madre Oriental and Occidental
mountains the mother mountains of Mexico
from Durango Chihuahua and Sonora
in moonlight in starlight in dumb silence
except for thudding hooves with the taste of rain
trembling in their mouths and pale morning
deepening red among the prairie-dog towns
and the last bawling calf complaining
wading the Rio Conchos and Rio Grande
trailing his boxcar mom
over the central plains of Texas and Kansas
across the Colorado Cimarron Snake and Missouri rivers
past villages of Comanche Sioux and Cheyenne
they travelled north
a white albino bull leading them
     Listen — you can hear them
     how the rifles boom
     and great beasts fall
     Long Tom and Remington
     and Sharps that shoots
     today
     from so far away
     it kills next month
     and prairie-dog towns
     are soaked in blood
     boom blor blam blum
     it's like a tune
     and death plays music
     from a thousand guns
     lead thuds and thuds
     into bawling calf
     and his boxcar mom
     and bearded bulls
     fall down fall down

It is hardly to be expected perhaps
by any except the most profound optimists
that any of the fifty millions
of buffalo will survive 1883
and vultures cruise overhead
they quarter the land in the sky
coyotes prowl on their flanks
and what god but an Indian one
would concern himself with life
or conceive a hidehunter's dream
of home and kids and cash
while a federal god in Washington
sits down and breaks bread
and gives thanks and cries
Bless You My Children
    The guns
    behind and on either side
    they bark and spit and howl
    a Springfield coughs and snarls
    the .50 Sharps goes boom
    an echo answers twice
    Long Tom aches in song
    and somebody far away
    hears death pass by in sleep
    hears death in a dream of life
    and blood gushes out
    blood gushes out
    beyond god's tourniquet
    (Hello there young lovers
    are you having a very good time
    in your antique beds and quite valuable
    patchwork shrouds circa 1880 now
    covering your wrinkled grandmother rotting bodies
    and your awful god-the-father and grandfather faces
    and God Bless Our Home somewhere
    adjacent to the kitchen smelling
    bacon frying eagerly
    adjusting his standards

to include a hoofed eschatology
among his part-time worshippers
true Christians?
Hello young lovers
travellers in an antique land
can you hear me?
acoustics here are lousy
but can you hear me?)
North of the Red River of the North
shaggy people of old time
to whom we prayed to be forgiven
for using their bodies for food
who seem not to be among us now
"for as long as grass grows
                    and water runs – "
They are moving north
steadily with a white bull leading them
but he is obviously there only
because of being a symbol
(buffalo tongue invoiced at 4-½¢ a pound)
Onward Christian Soldiers
to Blackfoot Crossing and Medicine Hat
And now a visit to the Cree Sundance ceremony
(to be re-enacted later
at considerable expense in Hollywood)
and now Mr. Mayor
among the quaint customs habitual
to our native peoples namely and to wit

the Woods Cree we may number one
we may number one you are about to witness
the Sundance
whose purpose is to make the buffalo immortal
manna so that Blackfoot Cree and Piegan
(those last named can't be trusted
being horse thieves from way back
so watch your watch Mr. Mayor)
may feast forever and their children
may feast forever on protein
which is to say an organism containing
at least half of 1 per cent of hydrogen carbon
nitrogen freq. also sulphur et cetera
Notice the buffalo skull centrally located
as it should be atop the tall pole
climbing a nether sky wherein we may locate
if so minded some primitive deity
identified with several other outmoded mythologies
but forgive me for being verbose
have a drink Mr. Mayor
The white bull
in 1883 moving north
west of the Red and north over the Assiniboine
at minus 4 Celcius across the Saskatchewan
and fifty million buffalo are following
Keep your eye on that white bull man
he's pregnantly meaningful
for us hidehunters and us coyotes

us Christians and vultures and whites and we'uns Indians
too and the bawling calf crossing over
Jordan – oops Saskatchewan River
obviously symbols of something
if we'uns can figure it out in time
Wide angle lens then zoom in fast
for closeup on that white bull sniffing rain
the very last time and you know what
(if you don't know what for chrissake
read the script read the gawdam script)
50,000,000 (fifty million) buffalo
last of the race till next time round
kinda genocide or buffalocide or like that
anyway they all find this big hole in the ground
a great cave the script locates near Battleford Sask
(you don't know about Battleford?
– it's a one-ford town in Canada
up around the Arctic Circle south of the Pole)
and there's thunder and lightning and all the elements
making a fuss and the script says Moses
which is the white bull with his people
Moses says Hello Young Lovers
whatcha doin tonight?
And then all them gawdam buffalo
why they just disappear in that hole in that ground
near Battleford – and I know I know
Battleford doesn't sound right not picturesque
so let's call it Pile-o-Bones let's call it –

time for lunch
Over the prairie-dog towns
blood-soaked holes in the world
buffalo thunder
to their cave in the earth
their wallow in the sky
−can you hear them Mr. Mayor
and you young lovers
also Blackfoot Cheyenne Arapaho and Cree
and even some white men
can you hear them down there
at the roots of the world
in the guts of yourself
a god in the ground?

no

THE HUNTING CAMP

Lost and wandering in circles
the camp seen for a third time
was like stubbing your toe
on a corpse
mouldy rotten logs an open grave
but the woods myth of continual circling
comfortingly verified as accurate
seemed a remote contact with warm human wisdom
It also seemed natural to address the trees
as a people substitute
but they would not speak
made no reply to his whispering yells
altho some were fat or thin
a few even looked a little friendly
but he told himself they were only trees
and said to them "You're only trees"
unsettled to hear himself
talking to a forest
That last time he saw the hunting camp
spectral with decay among the green life
something seemed to delay his own continuance
assuming continuance to be the sequence of thought
at least there was a gap in his life
he couldn't explain until afterwards
his last memory standing at an open tomb
which must have been the camp—then nothing
Afterwards
new-arriving bruises were evidence
of a few seconds when his brain had stopped
but feet had carried his mindless body forward
the forgotten feet slammed against trees
forest undergrowth whipped against his face
the feet bounced a body from tree to tree
and someone who was not his someone
had lived in his body during his death
then he re-occupied but without memory
only pain-evidence and a feeling of violation
his own thoughts beginning again and searching

for the stranger in his sixteen-year-old skull
In Hawk Junction distant as the moon
but only five miles away
he heard the trains' bodies shunting together
puzzled that sound came in waves and eddies
zig-zag voices that weren't there surrounding him
quite different from leaves touching other leaves
among which if you listened long enough
you might distinguish vegetable words
and he said to the leaves "What are you saying?"
In a clearing unaware of the sun
he might have seen a hairy man with humped shoulders
passing by intent on his own purposes
and wondered whether to ask directions
and wondered if he was capable of knowing
whether the thing was man or a bear
and felt pleasure at this intuition of instability
comforting as a pledge of fear of fear
Whatever time was went by
contracted or expanded somewhere in his skull
one thought went out to explore the brain's territory
among locked doors and doors slightly ajar
he kept arriving at blind alleys and places of no intention
—a second thought said trees had stopped speaking
a sub-thought said the trees had never spoken
but his thought concensus said they would someday
even tho trees were fat or thin but not human
trains actually were the hoarse voice of reality
Cooling sweat streaked his face and it pleased him
and the word for it pleased him: anodyne
which means release and solace from terror
he thought to make a song of it singing
and managing two syllables for every step
"O my darling O my darling Anodyne
You are lost and gone forever
dreadful sorry Anodyne"
and chuckled about the ridiculous sound
so exactly right for his regained calmness
then turning a street corner
in the forest found again
the hunting camp

ENGLISH FACULTY VERSUS STUDENTS
HOCKEY GAME
(At University of Manitoba, 1976 — in 1975
the students won, 9-2)

Sometimes looking at trees
or natural irregularities
and outcroppings of a hilly landscape
they seem like human figures
sometimes arms legs even faces
appear
       indistinctly
          purple
people of the twilight imagination

Okay I'll get back to that later
after the game if I remember
Bob Enright's blue beard bobbing
and I yelled Bob-Bob-Bob
fifty-year-old Arthur Adamson
skating zig-zag on zero to score
(ten years ago somebody says
his shadow was so fast it scored twice)
And the faces after we win
(7-6 and remember last year's 9-2)
the faces after the game of if
if I never see most of you again
and likely it's unlikely I will
not remember Art Adamson dancing
Bob Enright of CanStudies with tumult
dripping from his face in small drops
I will not remember Dave Williams charging
down ice like a night train into dawn
Now I meant to say there was a forest
in Dave—having led a poem by the nose here
for just that—but it's too damn silly
altho there was something I noticed
and can't remember and then remember
on the prairies there are no mountains

INSIDE THE MILL

It's a building where men are still working
thru sunlight and starlight and moonlight
despite the black holes plunging down
on their way to the roots of the earth
no danger exists for them
transparent as shadows they labour
in their manufacture of light

I've gone there lonely sometimes
the way I felt as a boy
and something lightened inside me
—old hands sift the dust that was flour
and the lumbering wagons returning
afloat in their pillar of shadows
as the great wheel turns the world

When you cross the doorway you feel them
when you cross the places they've been
there's a flutter of time in your heartbeat
of time going backward and forward
if you feel it and perhaps you don't
but it's voyaging backward and forward
on a gate in the sea of your mind

When the mill was torn down I went back there
birds fumed into fire at the place
a red sun beat hot in the stillness
they moved there transparent as morning
one illusion balanced another
as the dream holds the real in proportion
and the howl in our hearts to a sigh

PRE-SCHOOL

Black was first of all
the place I came from
frightened because I couldn't remember
where I'd been or was going to
But when I did find yellow
the gleam gold of things
first in buttercups and dandelions
Red was around that time
when I had to lie upsidedown
by the river waiting for something
to happen all one summer
while red willow roots waved
thru the water like a drowned girl's hair
I said as slowly as I could "You're red"
it was like happiness for the first time
and I agreed with myself
Dark colours came later
of course after the blue sky
brown takes study to like much
tho some of the brown kind of people
have silver lights in their eyes
from the time the moon left
here because of a promise
it gave the sun earlier on
and the brown people wanted to stay
in that gleaming landscape
and waited too long to leave:
in their minds they are not quite clear
they haven't dreamed their sleeping
why it was there were no shadows
in a country without colour
but silver silver silver

Later on
the house went smaller and smaller
and green moss grew on the shingles
then all the vegetable things in red and yellow
flowed orange and gold into women
and the grey child
went searching for one more colour
beyond blue eyes and brown hair
past the red tremble of leaves in October
and the silver women
the black awaiting us all

THE CHILDREN

By day
Chipewyan children scavenging
the garbage dump for food
Churchill housewives throw away
stuffing it into their mouths
as if they didn't remember how
and their rival scavengers
half-ton polar bears
slumbering down from the high Arctic
At the HBC store their parents
carting off boxes of garbage
by taxi and paying the driver
with social assistance money
At night children
in misery and boredom and hunger
wander the town
smashing shop windows
breaking into empty houses
the plague of Egypt in Churchill
platoons of children
ten-year-old privates
and twelve-year-old captains
creep thru shadowy backyards
raiding the white settlement
Joe says: no one watching
Elijah answers: now then
John says: burn it down
and their breath stops
a match flares bright blue
over Henry Hudson's sea glimmering
into a flame house
reflecting roof rafters of a sky

the white whale dreams under
the white whale dreams winter
sometimes John whispers to Elijah
but Elijah is dead
as droning taxis murmur
on the main drag of the town
Joe whispers to John
but John is too dead by then
and polar bears rear higher
than snow giants on the taiga
and white whale leaps across
the river-mouth till freeze-up
Joe whispers: where are you
and dung beetle taxis glide
past Chipewyan houses
trading booze for groceries
without one word spoken
under the smashed streetlights
ghost children
skip stones over the ice
and whispering to each other:
suppose the whole world
is a garbage dump
well just supposing it's so
and old tin cans are lovely
as pearls for a lovely princess
on the front of her lovely evening gown
and rotten spaghetti isn't
crawling white worms crawling
under the falling snow
that makes all things beautiful
Well just imagine just supposing
Mother Goose lived here
whispering stories to the dead children
about home sweet home on the garbage dump

for another million years
while Hickory Dickory Dock solemnly
concurs and Humpty Dumpty never
fell before Peter Rabbit became rabbit stew
and it isn't true
that Indian kids live like that
and die like that it isn't true
somebody's bound to say
besides it doesn't make a very good poem
and isn't pleasant either I guess
but to hell with poems
to hell with poems

Churchill

ODE TO A WORNOUT ELECTRIC STOVE IN THE SNOW

I've lived alone in my skin for leap years
outside the snow falls inside
the great barn of the world
and I notice philosophy
is impossible with no women
why is that?
I'm dangerously close to sanity
no social graces and no doubt eccentric
while six cusswords of querulous wind
penetrate bones and offal snow
covers all with white toiletpaper
and flagship cedars bend like pretzels
I have no philosophy for springtime
but out on the lawn that electric gimmick
sits reproachful
if there's a summer ever
the thing must go

TRANSVESTITE

Going naked into the snow
most unnaturally
        I mean why so silly?
I bet you never did that Julie
                or even in the rain
                    women don't
they must wear G-strings
and minimal make-up
because of the Apostle Paul
out there watching
But I'm trying to say why I
do things
        think like that
I can't
only there is an earth-power
in the lazy plunge and swirl of falling things
I don't know what it's for
and somewhere across the neighbourhood lake
a campfire rests against the curve of earth
and touching it the drifting snowflakes
make tiny spitting tasting sounds
I have lost and gained myself
rendered invisible
It's as if I were never here
        had never been at all
        nobody saw me
        tended my wounds
and I did prove I was never here finally
inside the sea inside the silent earth
separate and contained exploding inwardly
the body-clock ticks on
—going outside without
clothes into branching white
coral forests under a sky
surface so many miles over me
the Brobdingnags don't know
I'm here and the snowflakes falling
back to me are feathers
fused to my broken heartbeat
—so I regained this white plumage

RECIPE

Mostly Black Label beer but a few
exotics like Löwenbrau and Tuborg
some rum scotch and Szekszardi Voros
wine reminds me of Scheherezade in Hungary
Bull's Blood antidote for being alone
and Maxwell House coffee for chemical
balance all that celibate winter
I pissed in the backdoor snow
Come spring with fourteen suitcases
my wife arrives with a plague
of winged ants lording it at the backdoor
and she mentions accusingly those
ants are direct result of my unsanitary habits
—knowing these even in relative absence
I make the counter-claim (my only evidence
circumstantial) that pissing's beneficial
promotes world commerce and trade relations
open sesame street to the Common Market
That don't go down so good so
hot water unpromotes the ants' spring fever
boils some but the rest are lusty
I protest this action feebly but to no avail
For secretly and alone I've discovered the combo
to the Seven Cities of Cibola and Ponce
de Leon's life fountain obviously known to
Lazarus gushing alcohol at Ameliasburg:
now test-tube life is definitely out
for my urine formula raises
the dead satisfactorily and promptly
with Tuborg Black Label and Löwenbrau
and Scheherezade who's really Hungarian
It occurs to me that late this summer
we're planning a trip to Alberta driving
over bones of dinosaur monsters sealed
in silence seventy million years
—could it be possible?
—and then of course
the planets

DEPRIVATIONS

Stand quietly here
on the lake shore and fish
swim up in their lighted ballroom
at your feet doing a sundance
small bass so near transparency
they're nearly not here at all
but peering back from the other
side of becoming coming
closer closer very close
and I'm a thousand-foot
giant to them certainly not
supremely unnoticed not
less than nothing no
tear or blank spot
would suddenly appear
in the landscape
if I weren't there
but dozens of my selves
in their eyes would wink out
Among the fingerlings two
bullet-bodied cruising adults
drift dark with adult problems
—if there was a post office down there
they'd be leaning against it
if there's employment
they don't want to find it
they are incurably
fish and for that reason
a faint disturbing reproach
to whatever I am
I stand a few moments
in my aquarium of air
and they examine me
from their water incubator

a key turns somewhere
in a lock
now stops and stays here
and clouds are motionless
−to think that these
are prototypes of that first one
definitely weirdo and oddball
who dragged himself painfully
away from the salt waves
away from his quicksilver buddies
crawling up a gritty sand beach
for stubborn personal reasons
to set up dry housekeeping
and raise a family
I can't return there of course
have only this moment
of childlike rare communion
and sudden overwhelming envy
of things without the heritage
and handicap of good and evil
which they escape easily
with one flick of the tail
And something they do not know:
when I move my slowly stiffening
body and they scatter into diamonds
it is like a small meanness
of the spirit they are not capable of
and that is one difference

UPPER SILURIAN PERIOD

*(Characteristics: much of the land below the sea at first,
followed by mountain-building near the end. First
vertebrates noted in fossil record. On land, only ferns and
mosses and water. Approximate time: four hundred million
years before founding of the American Empire.)*

Look at the landscape – nothing there at all
only a cold grey mist
rolls heavily across sullen lowlands
but no ghosts of anything to terrify young girls
because there were no young girls
and nothing human had died to create ghosts from
– but there was something
at least its water potential
and the emptiness had a sad funny echo
in the long roll call of waves

However – in the glass house of water
Birkenia   Cephalaspis   Anglaspis
fish some six or eight inches long
Silurian mud grubbers and quite jawless
tho bone armoured for self-protection
against twelve-foot scorpions
(a kind of flesh-eating crab that was
rather evil – depending on your point of view)
that gobbled up the little warriors

An inhabitant of the later Pleistocene
– myself in the twentieth century
sitting with hand resting against my skull
tongue running thoughtfully over bone roof
of mouth while writing this poem
in a not-uncharacteristic attitude
– that bone a legacy of dermal bone armour
bequeathed by defensive-minded fish
over 400 millions of years

I have little advice for my own descendants
except perhaps to refrain from smoking
and excessive consumption of alcohol
(if such are available in the far future)
but there must be something
of tangible nature I can bequeath them
other than protective bone armour
some small thing of no practical value
such as writing poems
that may when ferns and mosses
and the monster scorpions rule again
serve to identify them
as harmless

SADNESS

—all wavery yellow and gold things
shining-across-the-windows-of-summer things
remind me of you
as well as old clichés about oil and water
however true
remind me also of the enormous load
of information and so-called wisdom
accumulated from the human past
which supplies no hint
or memory bank of ways and means
by which a man and woman
may live together
in a rented room
and looking back and ahead in all directions
notice nothing
except each other
except their fever
except their dying
as time continues
forever

SOUTH OF YUCATAN

I wanted to feel mnemonic magic
to be reminded of Quintana Roo in my bones
then a flock of green parrots overhead shitting
on the red Ford made me homesick
for the quaint charm of our outdoor privy
–take me back to old On-tare-eye-O

Quintana Roo

HOMAGE TO REE-SHARD

Frog music in the night
and all the dogs and cats and cows
on farms for miles in all directions
screech and howl and moo from shore to shore
the beasts of God bust their guts with song
and the sun a great bonfire burning away
darkness on the lake's little republic
but so delicate a rose tint on water
no girl has steps as light
Hockey—we have been talking hockey
Dave Williams and me at Roblin Lake
then slept and I wake him up later
to witness this birth this death of darkness
but how it relates to hockey—don't ask
tho maybe frog-music frog-music
of Montreal and Ree-shard the Rocket
"First madman in hockey" Dave says
not sensible and disciplined
but mad mad mad I see him
with balls shining out of his eyes
bursting a straitjacket of six Anglos
riding his back a thousand miles
of ice to beat the Anglo goalie
while all the dogs and cats and cows
from Toronto to Montreal and Roblin Lake
and Plains of Abraham forever
moo and screech and howl from shore
to morning shore in wild applause

The first madman
first out-and-out mad shit disturber
after cosmic duels with Bill Ezinicki
now sullen castrated paranoid Achilles
with sore heel in a Montreal pub retired

to muse on wrongs and plot revenge
with long memories of broken storefronts
along St. Catherine Street ·
when Maisonneuve's city made him emperor
for a day and hour and a moment
But Dave if I may interject a comment
difficult tho that may be
I think compared to the Rocket
all Iron Horses Catfish Shoeless Joes
and the Bambino's picayune meal of a mere
planetary dozen steaks and hotdogs and mammoth
bellyache sink to a minor tribal folk tale
in a trivial game of rounders somewhere south
"Hockey" says Dave pontifically
"is the game we're made of all our myth
of origins a million snot-nosed kids
on borrowed bob-skates batting lumps
of coal in Sask and Ont and Que
between two Eaton's catalogues in 1910
these are the heroes these the Alexanders
of our foetal pantheon and you know
you eastern bastards froze in darkness
you don't know Bill Cook and brother Bun
they came from my town Lac Vert Sask
they came each spring showering ice cream
and chocolate bars on all the kids
in my home town they were the new gods
almost replacing money
and you could see they knew
they were the gods..."

The sun now shines upon our right
out of the sea came he
for god's sake get ye hence to bed
no early risers we

And then I dreamed I dreamed Ree-shard
ancestor Maurice incestuous mythawful Rocket
standing at my bedside
I fled Him down the nights and down the days
I fled Him down the arches of the years
I fled Him down the labyrinthine ways
of my own mind—but he was too fast for me
his eyes blazing blowlamps
on Décarie and its cloacal hellway
and Montreal East kids with ragged *Canadien*
sweaters on St. Germain outside the factory
I worked in all the little Ree-shards
failing to negotiate contact
with their dream among the greasy-spoon
cafes and their out-of-work *peres*
and *meres* among the non-Anglos
among failed gangsters and busted drug peddlers
and '48 Pontiacs with bad lungs
coughing their own smoke in Montreal East
I dreamed Ree-shard and the kids
Me the failed athlete and failed lover
absurd idealist and successful cynic
I dreamed the bitter glory-fled old man
nursing his hate and grudges and memories
his balls making only sewer water
with Jung and Freud as solemn witnesses
But that man disappeared suddenly
and what took his place was the real thing
honest-injun Rocket indubitable Maurice
mad mad Ree-shard in fact the first and only
berserker astronaut among the lesser
groundlings their necessary flyboy
who slapped a star along Décarie hellway
and rang a bell in Bonaparte's tomb
and knocked a crumb from Antoinette's pastry
waved his wand at Anglos Howe and Ezinicki
and made Quebec Canadian

Rocket you'll never read this
but I wish for you all the best things
whatever those may be
grow fat drink beer live high off the hog
and may all your women be beautiful
as a black spot of light sailing among the planets
I wish it for just one reason
that watching you I know
all the things I knew I couldn't do
are unimportant

JEAN

I wrote such bad poems
when I was very young
when I was about fourteen
and thought poems were "poems"
instead of what they are
But some things I did then
with my self were poems
I used to walk with him
to the other side of town
in winter and stand outside
the house where a girl lived
stand silently maybe an hour
on Sundays or after school
hoping to see her
and never seeing her

Or confronting another boy
both of us about nine or ten
staring eye to eye
neither one backing down
but neither wanting to fight either
I can still see those kids
waiting
all that slow summer
of 1932 and still there
now slightly uneasy
about this poem

The dog died in 1933
but alive then and barking
with mad excitement
I had to hold his collar
to keep him inside
the yellowing snapshot
outside the quiet universe
of cats
My grandfather was old
twenty-seven years or so
older than Canada
with a big moustache
when we went hunting
crows with a shotgun
in an orchard of confetti
blossoms the gun boomed
announcing the coming
of a man of agricultural
aspect like God or my father
who approached bearing news
of amnesty for crows
I knew it was an orchard
because of all the apples
being born

Just because something is gone
doesn't make it a poem
but maybe the reason you remember
does

IN THE DARKNESS OF CITIES

How does one come to terms with the terrible beggars
staring straight at tourists near Minos' ruins say
or looking sideways at you in Oaxaca market as
if you held the only key to their survival in your pocket
and used it to unlock the door of a new Chevrolet?
I mean the very poor poor plentiful as money
things with withered breasts hands like claws
in Singapore and Karachi and mud huts in Yucatan
Indians scavenging garbage dumps behind factories
and how could you imagine their name is Mohawk say
Aztec Inca or anything proud enough to forget
their name ever meant anything except death?
I have a feeling about them sometimes
that they know all the books are nothing
and tall glass towers of cities and river bridges
and brains to harness the sun and moon tides
and send ships whooshing beyond the flowering earth
I have the feeling they know and know I know
that nothing in the world no feat or accomplishment
no riches from the ground or thought of men's minds
they know that nothing is ever done for them
no matter what extravagant words proclaim that it is
The fish is a thing only and we do not care
if it starves unless we need its body
the beast is slightly less of a thing for we know
we do need beasts' bodies to feed our own
and all other creatures merely supplement our own
existence each in its manner and for our benefit
But the poor are a needless luxury and they know it
they know the world would lose nothing if they left us
if they were squirted with liquid fire or disease and left us
alone on a solar tertiary adrift on our swaying raft
somewhere between nowhere and what might be someplace
    perhaps
and terribly they know this for I see it in their eyes
as I hold onto the lovely difficult money
the needful minimum sample of all good things

that seemed so necessary and worthwhile
and as I guard my little knowledge my precious thought
as I applaud the rocket cars motoring into absence
to explode in a dream on a picture tube somewhere else
they know our bright lights in the sky are not their lights
they know the beast is not fattened or the seed planted
for their harvest they know sun and moon are heat and cold
and mountain streams with deep amber coins in autumn
are not for them to spend on idle thoughts or beauty
they know
And in the face of their knowledge
all these mere words on paper
ring soundlessly in the vacuum of inattention
I know they mean nothing
as the terrible unaccusing poor know also
while brightly coloured birds
fly in and out from lonely caves of my imagination

SHALL WE GATHER AT THE RIVER
For Dave Williams

Riding a freight train for the first time
I was seventeen
and it rained
it rained like God was weeping
so hard he never noticed me
cowering in the shadow of his throne
When the steam rattletrap stopped
for water at Hawk Junction in NorOnt
I ripped the seal off a boxcar
trying to get inside out
of the rain and couldn't
budge the sliding door
Back on the flat car shivering
the CPR cop found me
and said I could get two years for my crime
and locked me in a barred caboose
to begin and end this sentence
I escaped (hardened criminal me)
and started to walk back to Sault Ste
Marie beside the tracks and figuring
that cop would be looking
stayed outa sight maybe thirty feet
inside the woods being fairly
cunning even at seventeen
Upshot was I outsmarted myself
got into the bush too far
lost in trees for two days
while it rained then it rained some more
For the last time in my life
I prayed and prayed some more
agnostically declining to take chances

Then very rationally I remembered the river
crossing under the tracks at Hawk Junction
river and tracks forming two sides of an isosceles
triangle so chances were two-to-one in my favour
that I could locate one of them
and did—I found the river
The question is: did God help?
I wondered afterwards
and answered my own question: NO
I worked out the problem alone
except for my friend Euclid
Years later another friend
(hearing this story)
has made me somewhat uneasy
and says "If there's a God
then the river was made by Him
rivers being part of nature
whereas the railway was man-made
and it would have been more in keeping
with your self-help theory
if you'd found the railway tracks instead
thus having no truck or trade with a possible God
Yes (my friend went on judicially)
it's too bad in a manner of speaking)
that you ever found that holy river"
All these long years later
my mind was quite at ease
now it chills my backbone
to think of that unprovable God
meeting me at the river
and saying nothing not a word
just sitting comfortably on his golden throne
the second-best one in muddy shallows
where little green gun-slingers
of frogs were shooting down bugs
and birds chasing desperate minnows

dive-bombed in the sudden sunlight
while God the scientist watched
observing a terrified boy
wandering thru hell
to rejoin the improbable world

ELEANOR

A trivial thing made me think of her:
we'd emptied out my old work room
so that it stopped being what it had been
I said "What'll we call it now?"
and neither of us knew

She is dead for seventeen years
but there is no name carved on the stone
because I had no money to pay for it
then altho I've made some since
—but she did have a name
Maybe three or four people have
shaped the word Eleanor in their minds
since — perhaps none and none
have visited the grave except me
not because they don't know where she is
they don't care and have no reason to
And that might be the point here
I don't either but feel vague guilt
because Eleanor isn't labelled on the stone
—as if I'd emptied a room in the house
of myself and it remained empty
If that sounds complicated you figure it out:
who names the stars
                    who tells the hours?
who calls the sun to stand at noon?
and conjures substance out of thought?
—all men are men and women women
unless you touch bodies with your hands?
—and they become
            Dear Human Dear Person Dear You?
—listen to breathing in an empty room of earth
                —who names Eleanor?

ALIVE OR NOT

It's like a story
because it takes so long to happen:

a block away on an Ottawa street
I see this woman about to fall
and she collapses slowly
in sections the way you read about
and there just might be time
for me to reach her
running as fast as I can
before her head hits the sidewalk
Of course it's my wife
I am running toward her now
and there is a certain amount of horror
a time lag in which other things happen
I can almost see flowers break into blossom
while I am running toward the woman
my wife it seems
orchids in the Brazilian jungle
exist like unprovable ideas
until a man in a pith helmet
steps on one and yells Eureka or something
—and while I am thinking about this
her body splashes on the street
her glasses fall broken beside her
with a musical sound under the traffic
and she is probably dead too
Of course I cradle her in my arms
a doll perhaps without life
while someone I do not know
signals a taxi
as the bystanders stare
What this means years later

as I grow older and older
is that I am still running toward her:
the woman falls very slowly
she is giving me more and more time
to reach her and make the grab
and each time each fall she may die
or not die and this will go on forever
this will go on forever and ever
As I grow older and older
my speed afoot increases
each time I am running and reach
the place before she falls every time
I am running too fast to stop
I run past her farther and farther
it's almost like a story
as an orchid dies in the Brazilian jungle
and there is a certain amount of horror

AT THE HOT GATES*

The boy is dead here
at the gateway to Greece
under jumbled heaps of dead
with guts mangled and eyes torn out
bodies in every direction
their garbage stench sickening my crewmen
All around us they lie
Assyrians in orange bronze with broken spears
Serangians toppled from their high-heeled boots
Thracians with fox-skin hats
Persians in dusty fish-scale armour
dead
And my brother's son under them somewhere
while a green sea hammers this coast
and the blue sea whispers beyond hearing
and the murky river pauses
on its journey from inland mountains
I have no heart to keep on searching
and boats from my ship await
while I think of the boy
dead in a far country
as Greece is a far country the last land
west for a dead boy under the heaped dead men
One rumour spreads that only a few soldiers
guarding this gateway to Greece
caused all the havoc
but that cannot be true
−or if it is true
what manner of men were those?
Our dead are numbered as the sands
crossed by Xerxes' army on the march from Asia
dead men scattered like stones on a stone coast
a dead army
multiplied by death and divided from life

Twenty thousand soldiers of the Great King
come to dust from a few Greeks
it is inconceivable
an ending lost to sight of the beginning
and my brother's son under it somewhere
with other sisters' sons and mothers' sons
first and last loves of women here
and the dead are equalled and exceeded
by those who loved them
under a bright Greek sky of deathly blue
so that twenty thousand girls with flowing hair
hover over the battlefield
in cloudy veils

*The battle at Thermopylae was in 480 BC. Three hundred Spartans and Greeks killed more than twenty thousand Persians. Xerxes, king of the Persians, ordered that their bodies be buried quickly, then allowed crewmen from his fleet to make a tour of the battlefield. However, as the Greek historian, Herodotus, notes, few were deceived in believing Thermopylae a victory for Xerxes.

RITUAL

A year in Winnipeg
and the great plain breathes
at my window outside the Red River
winds thru the prairie night
half a mile distant under snow
and the cold is not eastern cold
wolverine-sly
but claws and teeth of the bear
A year in Winnipeg
and after some months my personality retracts
that is – the reaching out to other people ends
I stand on a postage stamp
the past grows more attractive
today repeats tomorrow
and Mircea Eliade in uncanny mnemonics
remembers the birth of the world
for me in his books
and I have a nodding acquaintance
with Jung's unconscious
subconsciously appalled at breakfast
I am initiated into rites of the unbeliever
of history and repeat archetypal gestures
to the mirror and cut myself shaving
I've stopped venturing to Portage and Main
where drunk Indians and drunk whites
mix kaleidoscope colours
arthritic pain prevents such forays
except for beer and groceries
outside the university cage
My body ages swiftly
eyes are puffed and genitals limp
except sometimes awaking
from a dream of elsewhere
and sleep may come at mid-day
with a beer bottle

clutched in one hand
that I take on all journeys
and bring back later sometimes empty
I see myself dying in Eliade's creation myths
but none seem quite suitable for a writer
may die and be resusitated only in books
which of course are all my other selves
in illo tempore beyond my own time slightly
and my gods apart from Eliade's
are perhaps D.H. Lawrence and Dylan
or Henry Kelsey who explored the west in bad doggerel
their shamans are drunk Indians
reeling thru the dives on Portage Avenue
in any case Winnipeg is no town for T.S. Eliot
I am a solitary man
as such I certainly do repeat archetypes
and I can report various small household accidents
meals that achieve less taste than monotony
but nevertheless I eat and drink too damn much
even the typewriter that might seem extraordinary
in Eliade's canon has other practitioners
and their gestures obviously abolish time
and history as the religio-anthropologist
says archetypal things accomplish
and my "Person from Porlock" is the television set
The gods of course the gods of incandescent
moments do visit me occasionally
shrugging off the white Winnipeg world
that grows older approaching the new year
and I write and cook meals and grow older myself
in a cosmogonic myth of my own creation
as the sun climbs high at mid-day as the old moon wanes
as the Ford Galaxie corrodes as I cut myself shaving
and my blood flows into the bathroom sink
reaches the earth eventually reaches the rivers
and shines back at me in the sunset

UNCERTAINTIES*

Suppose there is
a woman so lovely
sunsets go unnoticed
and reflective lakes
become grey dishwater
—and while I think those thoughts
10,000 people die ⸻
in a Guatemala earthquake
and starving children
in Somalia go dreaming
into death as I indulge
my talent for trivia
Is that love
or a silly side-effect
emotional alcoholism?
And at what point
should one decide on
curative measures?
Do things sometimes
out of focus quiver
disbelief in anything
soberly suspended
and you kick yourself
in your sleep of reason
and say thank you
to the gods of wonder
for being wrong
about what's important?
As for her she is
nothing vocal
submerges saying
pre-emptive and emetic
of hunger and thirst
of other than her
-thoughts

night-gatherer
of luminous darkness
in images and patterns
but is herself
no pattern
is herself
But this word-jangle
and non-meeting of meanings
is semantic blind alley
to cite sonnet sunsets
like kidnap victims
from high school geographies
insufferable triteness
somehow penalizing
her who always in her going
out or coming forth
at noonday or evening
midnight and the dark hours
is one of those rare ones
in the instant of our summer
whose tomb is a birthplace

*The selection of love poems in this book (beginning with "Uncertainties" and
ending with "Subject/Object") was written from the possible viewpoints of
several other poets; those poets were named in the original and somewhat comic
titles. Those titles are now abandoned.

FROM THE WISCONSIN GLACIAL PERIOD

The rhythmic spell of insanity
begins again and I am not
myself but you are you
occurring to me from time
to time from Montreal
to Toronto
where I have an erection
350 miles long putting
to shame all the high risers
my dormant period ended
As I grow older
the aforementioned spell
of insanity seems
a rebirth of innocence
is like having a dozen lives
and where they intersect
stand all my selves watching
you in wonderment and crowd
around my lonely phallic cenotaph
Those long gold legs
your body transferred direct
from groves of white birch trees
and desert places of the mind
as just dessert
to my arms
—these are not the reasons
for my enslavement
tho definite considerations
but your eyes your eyes your eyes
so solemn so childlike so believing
I become your gentle worshipping anatomy student
given to biology geology and lethargy
guilty of ontology epistemology and misogyny
an old man new born an unbeliever
recently converted to timid prayer:

O flagellate bacilliform bacterial snot
suspended in limestone
pollen spores hitch-hiking thru the Pleistocene
cereal seeds dormant in glaciers
amino acid soup make a statement
of birth and rebirth of lechery
in fact say any damn thing quickly
gods give me strength
to repeat this particular moment
then repeat and repeat and remember

ANTENNA

Waiting:
everything in the city park super
real – trees   anonymous buildings nearby
are symbolic any-buildings at ten
below zero then the entire
background world just goes Phuutt
long pause then Phut more briefly
and can't be translated back – it
(the world) practically doesn't
exist except as something
to be stepped on crossing
Yonge Street in heavy traffic
to discover somebody's nose
is a cold rosebud and jumping
off a plane or taxi or rocket
at marsport drugstore the
unlucky martians almost human but
lack something fundamental for
instance not knowing
your thick pubic hair is
composed of a million tiny watch
springs inside an immortal hour glass
and one particular kind of look
is not yours alone but given to
a switchboard where little lights
flash or a bell tinkles
in the forehead answering
service announcing
an absence of before and after
but refuting that conjecture: a million
years ago in some forest
where happiness was not thinking
of anything but eating
someone before killing
his noonday meal and hurrying

thru the rustling silence
of himself must have
stumbled on this sadness
slightly similar to hunger
something he was the first
man capable of feeling
—and the woman knowing it
must have looked at him
a million years ago
questioningly

STOP WATCHING

You want everything
        everything there is
        but consider
how one sweep of the ballpoint mind
        makes it so
one chutzpah flourish and a mad florist
delivers ten thousand roses
the hard-sell salesman calls around
with Napoleon Brandy and a free Bentley
        Look I really am
sorry about my damned ebullience
and because you don't believe me
        Okay let's be sad
together follow the long curve of things
tracking deep space where we came from
in lives beyond our lives visiting
star graveyards—and our friends
stare sleepily and wave hello and the dog
that chased chickens comes yapping out
from the Milky Way silly with bitches
ridiculous aunts can be found young
when they were first becoming aunts
and cried and cried to be old
a new Hupmobile chugs among the comets
with two girls searching for London Ont.
lost in the month of August
We are sad sad
thinking of Jacko Onalik and Martin Senigak
two lost hunters in a blue snowmobile
searching for Sedna the seal-queen
searching for the undersea horizon
and consider Domenico Theotocopoulos
in the stained-glass shroud of Toledo
dead five hundred years

consider the two Scots runners
sent by their masters to explore Newfoundland
who followed the clouds who followed a snowflake
into the westland and somewhere
lost ones in their far away morning
of sadness brief as their lives
Then consider
how sadness translates to grandeur
in life as in literature
but summarized as grandiloquence
where bathos becomes soap opera
exaggeration winks understandingly at understatement
the clown mask crumples in laughter
translated as disbelief in anything
including ourselves as children
we inherit the world and each other
and we must be grateful for everything
while there is time

PAPER MATE

They meet in heavy snowstorms on streetcorners
muffled in thick overcoats and thermal underwear
– other storms storm thru their bodies
every snowflake is a cry
from not-meeting and never being
prompt for appointments of this nature
which are cancelled if not dealt with by proper authority

The proper authority for lovers is pain
they know each other's telephone voices
and joy-pain whispers over wires
not knowing they're fools is not enough
they must be aware of losing the whole blue world
which obviously amounts to nothing compared to each other
and break every phony vow for their sacred selves
of course moaning in near-agony and disbelieving
sensible advisers if any

Meeting in bare rooms and parks on aforementioned
wires everybody knows everybody guesses but trees
conspire like loyal slaves porch lights wink
out to hide them from themselves
day is reversed night dreams in all of us
but morning is a grey prophet when the angry god
of everyone arrives at noon to cast the first stone
– they are forced finally to ration the quantities
of self each gives and takes from the other
like medicine in teaspoons to cure themselves
from themselves but the malady is not susceptible
to standard treatment – only boredom is curative
they fear it and fear their own repeated necessities

Is magic then an everyday thing they say finally
is it sordid as tenements underhanded as rich men
can it be measured codified and shoved into time slots?
does it survive as itself or memory of itself
in absence or rare presence?
                              —it does survive however
all high points are loftier and depths much farther down
they find themselves alternately in clouds or dark caverns
(Jews and Arabs and the Irish Republican Army
indulge their different insanity somewhere in between)
and preoccupied with mapping the territory
they are in love with maps and charts of themselves
where a paper woman whispers to a paper man
"I love you" and he obedient "I love *you*"
and the phrase floats backward and forward
along the time lines among historic longitudes
where Troilus says to Cressida "He's a liar"
Beatrice to Dante "Let's hope so"
Nelson to Emma "Give them more rope"
and what'shisname that castrated monk
— Abelard plaintively "That sonuvabitch Plato
has much to answer for" (to Heloise)
In the opposite direction they hear us
but we don't hear them: our bedsprings musical
and ballpoints vociferous while some possible someone
might say wistfully "We are hostages to fortune"
—and science Great Science takes precedence over all
the High God of Genetics says "We're mortgaged to the future"
the living and the dying are a means before the end
but to paraphrase another whose name I've quite forgotten
"My dear oh my dear"

SUBJECT/OBJECT

What shall we say of these lovers
that has not been said of others?
Except—all doubt and self-derision
swept away even if temporarily
Except—mad wrestlers in the blood appeased
vampires refreshed from eating the god-selves
Except—reiterated personal signals
whose monotony and frequency are clichés
yes pure cliché remembering later
                    but yet also this
hard pride in defeat yes defeat by choice
submitting to apocalypse in a simple fuck
—a simple fuck?

Give me
the great ambitions
to scribble your name on a planet
to be a minus sign on the universe
yet be everything feel everything
obsessed with one single excellence
knowing
all these things sound trivial
when frozen to death on paper
to be what you are so fully
all questions become answers

Give me
chemical constituents of this dirty pair
of dogs grappling in some backyard
to reproduce more dogs   dogs stuck together
as panicky twin witnesses of themselves
morally responsible for their own predicament

Give me
the dictionary word and grunts and mutters
unthought sounds of fucking in bevel-aching ear
synchronized with blood and breath and bone
as fucking is the lost-and-found of love?

Give me
my guts return them immediately
subtract yourself from my self wholly
retract also your believable lies
                your crooked straightfulness
by mail or runner native to the country
and know that isn't possible
in lands beyond our lifetime
                the runners pull up lame

Give me
what you have already given
your own silence
balanced on the moment
in the waiting early morning
and the still air between us
the fullness and the emptying
this little place

THE COLOUR OF REALITY

You were lying in my arms
one hand running over all your soft smooth places
and this little girl kept looking in the window
I said "Scat, beat it, go find yourself
a nasty little boy to play with!"
—the kid disappeared in a big hurry
My hand walked into the anteroom
of where we had often come together
a place of warm gardens and bright blue thistles
disguised as forget-me-nots
"I won't see you again" you said suddenly
"For God's sake doesn't all this mean anything?"
I said angrily and opened my eyes
noticing your hair was a dull red colour
like a rusted piece of tin
and with an uncanny feeling
I thought—what the hell's going on here?

Awake
the correct video tape clicked into place
your hair once more a bright yellow
—but the desolation remains
I can hardly bear it being even a dream
and think—what if all those other times...

BORDERLANDS

No way of knowing where we went
on those long journeys
Sometimes there was a whiteness
as of snow that obscured everything
but it wasn't snow
Sometimes it seemed we left a campfire
and looking for it again
couldn't even find the burned place
blundering into trees and buildings
—but then nothing
has ever confused me as much as light
Sometimes we arrived back separately
but still seemed inside the borders
we crossed by accident
and want to be there if we think it real
but we do not think it real
There is one memory
of you smiling in the darkness
and the smile has shaped the air
                    around your face
someone you met in a dream
has dreamed you waking

TURKISH DELIGHT

Strange towns I like on accounta
I can't predict the lady
tiger lurking around Ionian
corners where beer is awful and camels
fart all night long strange
music of the mod east and nesting
storks perch atop columns
of tenth-century Byzantine masonry
and Allah speaks daily
from a tape recorder
then past the shops a corpse borne
shoulder-high by friends
of corpses down the unpronounceable
street my backbone ice and small
wind-devils swirl like grey pots
of flowers and dark solemn pall
-bearers looking not right and not
left behind by the deceased
but one staring straight
at me his round holes of eyes
saying nothing but stating complete
zero xeroxed in me caught
somehow in their net of grief relieved
to discover kids on another street
—one dirt-smudged small girl smiled
at me and I smiled back
my shivering foreign smile
a bright pause that went on and on
until she ran thru the dust
to tell her mother all

about how I had smiled and watched
and went and how funny-odd
it all was in a strange town around
the grave-corner from here
with a name like futz or something
similar where Turkish camels fart
soundlessly forever in my mind it recurs
and well I have been finding out
for years and years what
it's like to be alive
before it stops

Turkey

PROPER ARRANGEMENTS IN COLOUR AND SOUND
(The CIA raises a sunken Russian sub in 1974)

Aware that the salvage operation would
also raise the bodies of the dead Russian
officers and men, the CIA had made what
it felt was the proper arrangements.
The Glomar Explorer was equipped with
special cooling facilities that could
accomodate up to 100 corpses. In the
forward section of the submarine were
a number of bodies. While a loudspeaker
played a recording of the Soviet national
anthem, a funeral service was read in
Russian and English. As the CIA camerman
filmed the proceedings in colour
and sound, the bodies were buried at
sea from the Glomar Explorer, each
neatly shrouded in canvas.

R.I.P.

found in Time *Magazine, March 31, 1975*

INFANT MONSTER

From the high plateau of Anadolu
some 10,000 feet above sea level
a baby wild boar
about the size of a teddy bear
leashed to his moustached master
And the little grunter is stubborn
wants to go his own way
squeals angrily at the moustache
who yanks him back choking
but a moment's lapse of attention
and he heads for the hills
Hard to reconcile this brown toy
on the streets of a big city
with the full-grown monster charging
thru highlands near Mount Ararat
built like a brick thundercloud
with tusks to uproot a railway
or sink a medium-size destroyer
Down the hot street they go
a little brown pig and an old man
squealing and yanking
with neither being exactly sure
who leads and who follows
or what either would be doing tonight
if the choice could be made alone
if the choice could be made at all

Turkey

IMAGINE THE ANDES

Imagine a Cadillac
or Rolls in the Andes Mountains
chauffeur-driven with a millionaire
in the back seat smoking a cigar
and fondling his mistress
in touch with London and New York
by radio telephone
following the wild Urubamba
to headwaters of the Amazon River
thru high places of less than silence
where in the beginning there was no word
not even absence which might indicate
God was having trouble with language
—imagine the Andes

All you see are old Fords or Volkswagens
decrepit from switchback roads
because the Andes make everything
shrivel beside them
autos age like people and no proud Caddy
would even speak to a dog-eared Chevy
nor an ambling shabby llama
climbing a mountain at Machu Picchu
a Plymouth applies for the old age pension
Mercurys are on social assistance
Austins gasp from the altitude
mountains are not deluded
by external combustion

Imagine Hitler in the Andes
fled from his burning bunker
while goose-stepping legions
clomp the *altiplano*
a military *non sequitur*

Pizarro's aging *conquistadores*
a murmur of plunging echoes
Stalin Napoleon Caesar Alexander
demonstrate inadequacies of the phalanx
It's impossible to visualize
like trying to know another person
you cannot
flesh and bone and soaring
peaks defeat you
Inca descendants are your only
close approach and they more
enigmatic than their birthplace
for mountains are like convoluted
brains with kings inside the stone
and vultures patrolling
the wind's four quarters
I think they do not see me
at all and yet see everything
Imagine the Andes

Machu Picchu

CANADIAN SPRING

Forests are dark and leafless in March
the morning sun then hesitates then peers
around its own lessening shadows
where brown grass has green memories
But there's some mistake
— by afternoon the day darkens
again and water deliberately
assumes its icy alter-ego
Spring is a series of advances
and retreats but always
edging farther toward the sun
and you think how terrible
it is to be trapped
in a perpetual graveyard
where everyone looks at everybody with pity
or fury if they luckily escape

That dark forest is superimposed
on the Gringo Trail where I'm wandering
in Peru and Pachacuti the Inca conqueror
alternates with Big Bear and Crowfoot
in my mind mangos are puritanically illegal
and grenadines a sexual aberration they
emerge from piles of dirty snow
in Canada but llamas on the *altiplano*
too morally superior for enthusiasm
about anything much less human beings
pause for the camera
whose reverse image is rabbits preparing
for survival by doing and doing
what rabbits do best here
Machu Picchu slumbers another thousand years

Advance and retreat retreat and advance
spring comes sideways spring comes slowly
lilacs imagine their colour is purple
trilliums make up their minds to be white
tolling winter hesitates at street corners
ding-dong spring is silent temporarily
but people are less unpleasant to each other
bars on the prison widen slightly
to re-admit escapees and mayflowers
— my collar is a fuse to prevent strong feelings
my life has a tourniquet holding back freedom—
but rivers slash their wrists
a thousand rivers roar one instant only
sea-wide forests fill the near horizon
forests are banners sprawling green
birds build nests inside this one-time prison
birds are coloured bells
—and it's summer

Cuzco

SIDEWALK BEER GARDEN

Traffic roars high above the tolerance level
my wife and I sit under an awning
me drinking beer she buying roses
from one of the many hovering flower sellers
both resting from bad trips on the Gringo Trail
Anyway this car stops and double parks
an old fat man emerges and hobbles to a table
is met by a slick young guy with a briefcase
my guess is some kind of small business deal
for Briefcase acts like a flunkey
The fat man altho dressed like one of the boys
is obviously rich and his car a Mercedes
the chauffeur waits inside as traffic flows
respectfully around and nobody even honks
Making furtive derisive gestures to each other
the flower sellers are scornful of all rich men
and this archetypal one particularly
but not money itself of course
I am taking it all in like writing a novel
aloud to my wife when along comes a part-Indian beggar
as beggars go this one is the last word in bums
a horror of rags and dirt and bare-assed
we give him some money and he staggers off
without dignity or pride or seeming to need them
"Now that's odd" I say to my wife
"The guy at the next table is rich as Rockefeller
owns a Mercedes and has a chauffeur waiting
so why didn't our beggar panhandle the rich guy?"
"He knew better" my wife says from her roses
Whereat I am dumbstruck by this quality
of wisdom in women denied to husbands
in fact I am humbled even tho not very long
for now around the rich guy and his huckster
one can discern vague outlines of a barricade

erected around the two repelling all but servants
perhaps similar to the aura Pilate saw around Christ
whereby all men are identified for what they are
as apart from surface appearances
And glancing at my wife who is not unusual
in appearance waiting for me to finish the beer
I can't quite put my finger on something
extraordinary about this trivial incident
involving all of us
in the land of the proud Incas
and it scares hell outa me

Lima

SEPARATION

Then neither of us will see the other die
no oozing tears and pity
the close watching
wondering who's first

It will happen some place else
one of us will know later
among the crises of blurred eyesight
constipation and insomnia

A sick old woman a sick old man
spared something
spared pain and unnecessary grief
spared love

THE DIVORCED WIFE

—divorced from plain honesty and integrity
qualities for which I am justly famed—
this reprehensible act of deceiving your husband
—centuries will lapse before I forgive you
for plain woman's treachery
Long having paid for your various misdemeanors
with hard-earned poet's cash
you present me with the squalling child
of your secret endeavours to please
someone who isn't me in this case
the repetitive god of Photography
and one photograph so like a painting
I can't tell the difference
Not that it's necessarily good
I mean the colours are phony
the old ship in a glass bottle trick
and she in her years with me has only
in the marital sense ever been a sailor
Moreover I'm now quite jealous
the woman has done something impossible
for me because I can't embarrass her
by excelling a woman quite casually
as if to say stick to home and babies
cleave to the dominant male
stop making coloured paper miracles
begin to explore the nearest planet again
stop loving me
in surrogate effigy

ARTIFACT

Dull red-pitted stone
maybe granite
shaped like a loaf of bread
found in the backyard
flanged at top and bottom
but it might be upsidedown
maybe six inches long
but I didn't measure
that would make it captive
Anyway it could have been
footwarmer for nineteenth-century settlers
corn grinder after the last ice age
something Indian women used
for husbands to stub their toes on
So I took the question to Toronto
and it damn near broke my briefcase
kept straining my arm muscles
a stone heart at my fingertips
I showed the thing to various experts
at ROM and Canadiana places
but there was always one expert more
the guy I didn't get to see
the guy with degrees supposed to know
glance at me superciliously and say
grandly "This is *trichonosis flamboyatis*
—in layman's terms a twillig fork"
I never caught up with him
he was always eating his sabbatical or something
there was always one expert more
I got disgusted carrying that red heart
around ROM lugging it thru mammoth bones
corridors of snooty Egyptian mummies
so that now it stays home
I don't know exactly where
but it wanders free as a lost key

I'll never identify it completely
can say only it belongs in some ghostly household
no doubt had sweat fall on it
was picked up and hefted and dropped
on somebody's toes most likely
and among all the household articles here
I can be sure it's the only one
bound to survive another thousand years
identical as the identical thought
it came from
It's what we all come to I guess
the basic thing under froth and flesh
commonplace and mysterious
at which words end helpless
unable to follow the thing farther
speculation ends at the same wall
I dont even want to know what it is
or find that last expert eating artichokes
at the Four Seasons the sonuvabitch
might tell me but I know
he doesn't know it's a gift
from governments of stone

MURDER OF D'ARCY McGEE

1   1868

The murder was just past
Metcalfe on Sparks Street
at Mrs. Trotter's boarding house
– dark early morning in Washington
Troy or Medicine Hat or London
and two drunks huddle close together
one dead one weeping

The big full moon a silver orange
toppled houses into shadows
near the body a half-smoked cigar
some blood and McGee's new hat
his wife bought last week
everything was evidence
The kneeling man crying
he was a friend naturally
at Mrs. Trotter's boarding house
located finally in Ottawa
it might as well be
not New York or London
but it was April

Shadows shadowing a shadow
after a horror movie long ago
let's kill the bastard they said
when we were all unborn
and murder an old habit
Death resulted from a Smith & Wesson
bullet –: last night in his last speech
he rested one leg on a chair
because it hurt less that way
and talked about a new country
one more among the many
The killer may have been Whelan
anyway they hanged him for it
he was a tailor

2   100 YEARS LATER
News Item: McGee Murder Weapon Discovered

Mrs. Trotter's boarding house is down
skyjacked planes fly round the world
nobody knows who kidnapped whom
—why just the other day Vermeer
was snatched from his museum wall
garbage drowns low-hanging clouds
nothing has changed that I'm aware

Why then McGee?
I mean why mention things like this at all?
—while moss creeps over all we know
and cries we made are whispers soon
a dead man rots in Montreal
happy enough and so are we
The wife and friend are dead as well
(the friend of course was Whiskey John
Macdonald): the country sleeps so sound
that sleep is death apparently
while ivy grows the clock ticks on
—only some lovers break the spell
and dream their children into birth
and fancy that the world is theirs:
—what town what country and what world?

In Ottawa old buildings lean
against the earth in afternoon
with the look of waiters tired of standing
and when we've all grown tired of it

we stay in bed a little longer
to read detective stories
The headlines shout
ballistics say
Whelan may be innocent
– don't look at me
for I don't know
how can I tell who's innocent
the experts speak and I am still
but everything is evidence
in verse sometimes or deathless prose
and murders happen more than once
In Cote des Neiges Cemetery
the bald detective lurking in forget-me-nots
slips handcuffs on a skeleton

RODEO

Inside the Stockmen's Hall drinking
beer with Marvin Paul who looks
like a tragic poet and carves totem poles
taking three weeks to earn four dollars
Outside in the dusty arena horses explode
with arched backs and William Billy Boy
sails upward in air and downward to dust
Another bronco refuses to do anything at all
just stands there somewhat reminding me
of a friend saying "it's better not to be born"
There is free will it seems here in the Chilcotin
a semi-circle of mountains stares at the sun
an old Indian with his face a dark forest
outside the Stockmen's Hall sleeps tenderly
I am waiting with Marvin Paul for one of those
moments when all will be made plain
to me when the calf-ropers build their loops
and lasso the stars as William Billy Boy rides
to his inheritance on earth in eighteen seconds flat
his own people quiet and the whites noisy
while our round earth resumes colloquy with the gods
As things stand now Marvin Paul incoherent
with beer sells me his pencil portrait
which translates him to a tragic dimension
the wild cow-milkers clutching beer bottles
strain for a few drops but the beasts refuse
William Billy Boy is slammed to the dust
his bent back aches and he won't ride for awhile
Nothing is finally made plain to me
but I have stated my intention set the scene
the same one in which a bored housewife
prays for a romantic lover and the bankrupt rancher
stares at his parched range and starving cattle and spits
both settle for less than their dreams: the woman for a man
the rancher for one more year in the high Chilcotin
myself for something less tangible
hovering in my mind close to this poem

STOPPING HERE

The little skeletons of rabbits
run with their fur still outside them
Animals don't sweat do they?
— but I was sweating and running
from the orchard after stealing apples
I never won anything

Always envied the birds when I got caught
being slow and terrified and hard
of hearing when someone yelled Stop
I kept on going somewhere

Was I running from or towards?
— rabbits haunt me with their breathing
guns crack in icy fields beyond the town
on market days the farmers sold their bodies
— it must have been from something

Chickens with their heads cut off still run
an axe leans softly in the backyard
the man said chickens don't know anything
but they do don't they?

I fell down sometimes and panted
on the earth and sky leaned up
to cover me with feathers
whatever touched me didn't know my name

DOORS

The lake carries music and voices
to me, by an acoustic trick
I don't understand. Of course,
easy to get scientific explanations.
But I don't require them. At this point
I realize I understand nothing.
The music like glass shattering,
and not pleasant, is still a gift
from the night. Those shattering voices
muted slightly, come from a certainty
they don't understand either, but perhaps
think they do. Beyond music – other voices
where that certainty resides, immense contemplative,
and is itself nameless. Perhaps at such moments
something enters or withdraws from the room,
one bar of music, the exact one, escapes
from the makers to join dissonance: it rings
against my life, my life it seems
I have misunderstood always, but always
waiting knowing a certainty does exist,
as when you enter or leave any place
that I am with an ordinary smile,
beyond the voices beyond the music
a small sound flows with you,
that is not you, or of you,
but knows you –
and I listen

NIGHT SUMMER

Music imitates words sometimes,
as if on carbon paper
or thru thin tissue of sound;
and even with no words written
for it, a meaning passes by
the doors of rooms and gestures
for you to follow...
But sometimes without words and meaning,
the sound drags no things behind it,
not love tho perhaps lovely,
not a fall but maybe falling,
no given summer but any one.
Then again there is a music
that is complete forgiveness
for being, and does not ask or take,
makes no promises whatever,
an experience beyond even the music
that made it possible once.
Listen to it again and all is different,
as if the listener added one of his selves
before, and the self-music takes the listener
to a mountain peak where a man sits writing
—not music, not words, nothing
that can be taken away,
touched, handled, lifted, fingered, tasted,
not to be known unless the lost self
aches, the man remaining severed
from what he was, knowing
the sadness of that other self,
of all that ever lived and is
ending with a sigh....

CREATIVE WRITING CLASS

You do not fit the mosaic
an odd-shaped piece of awkwardness
falling into no category
a character formed principally
from rejection of other values
and the brief fashion of whim
Taking no particular pride in this
out-of-step off-key drummer
beating sardonic pain rhythms
deciding there is no help
for your own unmalleable rigidity
But click
a sympathy vibrates a likeness
astonishes inside the tangled candelabra
of laws the sculptured simulacrum
ugliness of minds born from a mud matrix
among mysterious hows and whys
and mish-mash sundaes of weekends
tentative logic of these
an awareness you have not joined
but wait at some crossroads
where cars flash with neon red
assholes and a small moon moves
inside the ballet of raindrops

PLACE OF FIRE

There are smokestacks hundreds
of feet high, disciplined phallic
chimneys penetrating the helpless sky
in ritual rape, towering above dead bodies
of factories. But technology built them —
I mean, they're too cosmic to be personal.
Ours is twenty feet. And still climbing.
Ingredients: limestone from an 1840 regency cottage
(I told Bill Knox he was nuts to tear it down);
historic stone from the Roblin gristmill site;
anonymous stone from Norris Whitney's barnyard;
and some pickup loads from Point Anne quarry.
— All this to toast marshmallows?

But you'll have to admit the ritual significance
of not being above working with your hands?
You don't admit? Okay, I guess you're right.
But you must agree it's the hard way
to gather ingredients for a poem?
— lugging tons of $CaCo_2$ stone plus fossils?
Symbolic as hell too: you can't beat limestone,
which Auden said was very important stuff;
W. Yeats and R. Jeffers kept building towers as well,
so they could write great poems about it.
I'm just the latest heir of this hearth-warming
tradition, eh?

You know, I've talked myself into a corner:
it would be silly now to mention that at my shoulder
the dark tribes are hovering and worshipping,
stone people who preceded the jukebox people;
and before them the first fossil critters,
having such a nice trip in their stone coffins.
I won't mention them. That would be too much.

I did forget to include the inheritors bit,
mystic stuff about hearing whispers from the far
past, me a listening lowly high priest,
unacknowledged legislator or something—
Of course what I'm actually doing, or seeming to,
is telling anyone reading this how to write a poem:
so build your fireplace, raise your stone tower,
fall in love, live a life, smell a flower,
throw a football, date a blonde, dig a grave
—in fact, do any damn thing, but act quickly!
Go ahead. You've got the kit.

GROUP PHOTOGRAPH
1935

He had a face like an emperor
when we lined up for the team picture
perfectly handsome and self-possessed
(and the self is an uneasy thing to possess)
the others gap-toothed and ill-at-ease
                            but in their way perfect
because of time because most of them are dead
and as much because of something lacking
as the fake symmetry of their arranged bodies

When I was flat on my back looking at clouds
he was squiring girls and figuring angles
with less money his wits were sharper
and he did fiercely well at everything —
he was the whisky sunlight he was the speaking rain
I listened to and he needed listeners
and of course he was my friend
me the slow and lumbering team centre
without any ferocity at all

Once playing Madoc he took the hand-off
from Vanderwater (who kept farting in the huddle)
and danced with four Madoc men literally danced
and grinned at them sympathetically before scoring
— and their drunk fullback slammed into me
a hard three times mindlessly and mindlessly
I stood there and met him unable to fall
he swiftly sober and me suddenly drunken
while girls on the sidelines giggled

Later he soared above the war in a bomber
flying officer then flight looey he took me for a flip
me the corporal me the summer witness
upside down in the fields of noon
looking for something I never found
with summer nearly ending
he went overseas I stayed at Trenton
men kept dying
and I was soon a civilian

Afterwards he stayed in the service
stationed in Egypt (myself in the taxi business)
his emperor face unlined but his wavy hair
totally disappeared and brilliance a little thin
but if you're looking for a big put-down
here in what I'm saying there won't be one
it's just that something actually was lacking
and he knew it and it haunted him
but how wonderful not to be perfect – ?

In the late fifties he crashed a civilian
training plane in Oshawa nearly
anonymous then as a flying instructor
and my friend died quickly
There's not much to be said
about a man's life
that is rarely anything but meaningless
except that what this man didn't achieve
no longer seems important
and what I owe him
is

THE STATUE IN BELLEVILLE

A mid-size town with the usual quota
of graft and politicians opening bridges
of which it has three including a footbridge
You could say it's still Victorian
because it's very quiet because it's respectable
with shops and poolrooms but no whorehouses
at least they don't advertise
Once it also had Mackenzie Bowell
who got to be Prime Minister in 1895
nobody knows why but the statue on Bridge Street
near the armouries the little man stands

The little man stands where soldiers drill
sometimes people forget but birds remember
to stop at "The Fixer" the man you went to
if you weren't a Catholic for a job
or favour of some kind or other
—when he was Grand Master of the Orange Order
cock of the walk in Belleville when Belleville
was something and Belleville was something
in winter the northern lights were something
and threw up a silver grandstand in the sky
and poor boys got to be PM by working
hard and after all he did know John A.
after all was that statue

When Bowell was PM and the Dogans downtrodden
came a day when The Fixer was fixed himself
Said Mackenzie Bowell "I must reverse my field
and supporting the Dogans I'll stay PM
because Manitoba Dogans live somewhere near China
but I must have their votes their votes I must have—"
When seven mad cabinet ministers called at his house
and said resign or else or else just resign sir

Mackenzie Bowell called em "a nest of traitors" he did
—those dirty doublecrossing bastards
he thought unforgivingly and went to church
and at Bridge Street United for being a sonuvabitch
forgave himself quite readily

It's still a town where you really can't tell
small men from big men — Belleville I mean —
poor boys work hard and maybe some fixers
for parking tickets industrial zoning and tips
about the location for our new shopping plaza
and I should have more faith in our democratic system
But maybe I left out part of this story
because if evil is penalized and good rewarded
there'd still at Old Home Week be hardly any people
Which is to say Belleville is a mid-size town
with mid-size people medium virtue among us
you know there are comparatively few heroes
except The Fixer — he's the best I can do
and some of us feel we couldn't do any better
times bein what they are and so if you don't mind
let's raise a cheer

TEN THOUSAND PIANOS

The Arctic is mostly silent in summer
seals bark only at a distance
from the rifle's mean crack
or a motor's stutter
breaking the blue glass of water
In evening ducks mourn
eerily their fate as ducks
the killer whale ghosting along
hiding beneath a dorsal fin
soundless as words on paper
Idling past a mile-wide iceberg
in the canoe listening
to meltwater dripping in the sea
ice marries itself to water
as red leaves float down in fall
as snow or rain or lost words
wandering beyond hearing
Listen to your blood negotiate
interior roads in the brain's back country
or lying on your back in grass
clouds buffet clouds in leaning silence
under the upsidedown mountains
I am an elderly boy come here
to take piano lessons
realizing one should be born
in silence like a prolonged waiting
after the first death-cry
knowing this music
is what silence is for
in a canoe in Cumberland Sound
waiting among the white islands
for summer's slow departure

Baffin Island

HERO

Over the humpbacked ice I drive my dogs
hunger-mad and sucking salt blood
from my wrists drinking it instead of tea
but rushing desperately-needed supplies
to the starving fiord people

On arrival they cheer loudly
as the last ice age glacier
breaking off into the sea
I'm enshrined in their mythology and smile
beyond their birth behind their faces
my expression ennobled by suffering
and those who approach me are better for it

Of course I claim all this is fantasy
but there are those present who say it happened
and crowd loudly around with their congratulations
despite token protest on my part
After a while I accept homage
for it would be ungracious to refuse
nagging doubts quiet
knowing I have come at last
into my kingdom

For I believe it now: the running man
beside the sled
parka icicled like a helmet in the disappearing sun
honour hovering in his white breath and breathing
his name constitutes an awed prayer
on lips of all beholders
—that man was me

SNAPSHOT FROM BAFFIN ISLAND

Father Danielo RC priest at Pond Inlet
among Eskimos in the high Arctic:
"I've made one convert in twenty years"
The snapshot shows him a little shrunken
man wondering if his life was wasted
and dying shortly after the picture was taken
Of course Pond Inlet is Anglican country
they had first crack at the heathen Eskimo
who now have names like Jonahsee and Leah
or Mosesee right from the Old Testament
But one must have resisted the Anglican hard sell
and driving his skidoo over endless icefields
he remembers dead Father Danielo
distributing oranges and apples
a gift from his iron god of warm weather
among the trembling snowflakes

KERAMEIKOS CEMETERY

So old that only traces of death remain
for death is broken with the broken stones
as if convivial party-goers came
and talked so long to friends they stayed
to hear the night birds call their children home

All over Athens rooster voices wake
the past converses with itself and time
is like a plow that turns up yesterday
I move and all around—the marketplace
where something tugs my sleeve as I go by

Greece

SUCCESS STORY

When I came down from a rural town
to Yorkville by the sea
I drank ten aspirins in my coke
after a couple of months I woke
then back on Mother Parker's tea
When sniffing glue was the newest craze
I stuck to the toilet seat for days
but felt a little behind the times
humiliated so to speak
by some of the walls I couldn't climb
and started chewing poppy seeds
then nothing salutary as pot
could in the grocery stores be bought
and emerged from an acid anal trip
with a psychedelic post-nasal drip
Then nutmeg became the thing to chew
considerably stronger than airplane glue
except my chick had turned quite green
so we had to wait and not resume
our trips till both drank Listerine
and then went back to the Yorkville scene
Now that living is nearly a crime
and the fuzz are onto us all the time
a breeze from the big American draft
has turned me into a quiet man
my chick and I have both left town
there's nothing here but sheep and cows
we're down on the farm without one dime
where the wild grapes grow and making wine

COYOTES IN MERIDA ZOO

Hey you needle noses and wire whiskers why can't I be natural as you
without pre-planning my face split wide as a toothpaste ad
in the haunted jungles of Yucatan?
Especially the kid coyote frolicking frisking grinning snapping maw
he says listen maw tell me ain't I the best damn nonesuch baby coyote that ever was maw
pay some attention borrow me your ears I'm gonna bite your nose
chew your tail in fact I'm gonna climb all over you with so much love
under sideways and back again as close to incest as water melts into rain
and a rainbow leaps from colour to colour in puppyhell and heaven
he says maw ain't I marvellous ain't I intelligent
not knowing I know nothing *mama mia* baby mine I don't need to know
nothin on accounta you're a pinball machine and I'm gonna play you this kid
gets exactly what he wants without knowing what this kid wants hey?

The broad-cheeked watching Indian faces are impassive
at all this excess of life needless exuberance they guard themselves deep
inside themselves like smouldering fires only occasionally leaping
to open flame in a country where heat slows down everything except death
Spanish-blood people are mildly amused
they've read books and some of them see those books in coyote faces
some see beards and leather bindings some see Freud and Jung in consultation
and everything verifies everything they almost expected
and were afraid to anticipate unless it might not happen

Ol man coyote well he don't go for this consarned nonsense that damn forward pup
wa'l he bustin his britches anyways pop couldn't get away with such goins on
himself the old man's jealous leastways he acts offended his *amor propre*
demands he break into this closed circle of mutual admiration like
he desires maw to say hey you big ol silly ol he sonuvabitch
why don't you unwrap me like a parcel layer after layer and bellyhell
of fur and fun and thoughts of what I am which is female most like why don't you
investigate that for a change of venue instead of fleas maybe even outside mating season
beyond this silly pup we made
together once when the moon hammered our only possible prison bars
in black parallel rows on the sky-seeking hills of Yucatan?
The old man don't say a thing
then he has this bright idea and starts to chase his tail
the ol man goes round and round so famously furiously ephemeral ephemerae he blurs
he actually do but the cosmos wow hurray the cosmos
blinks he say look at me boy ain't I sumpin
to see I can do anything you can do I can do better you young last half squirt
you're gonna be sorry you took on the old man
why kid you just watch my speed see it takes a better pup
nor you to get the best of this the best damn go-go dancer in Yucatan

The new-created vacuum of speed drags half the city and all myself
in the mad coyotes' wake me trotting in sleep and spinning in heavy circles
around a hairless ape and chasing my vanished tail nostalgically
thinking migawd you know there's coyotes I like better'n people
thinking migawd there's people who oughta be coyotes
thinking migawd you couldn't invent this scene you didn't set this stage it's thought
set to music it's the chromosome dance it's blobs of what matters
balancing on their tails it's what never was
or could be never if there wasn't a world not unlike this one
an opposite world to mud and blood and ugliness in the heart of Yucatan
and three crazy coyotes I suddenly love like new-born love hey
and for me the balance quickly tips my plus factor rediscovered and pronto
a free bonus for enduring life rich reward for having invented my own particular world
At this point maw and the kid why they watch kinda amazed with pity they wanta be noticed
they say you poor ol guy who oughta retire you're gonna have a real bad coronary
because you ain't really one of Saturn's rings really no yo-yo you
come back to earth now hear real quick instead of spinning and changing hands
to make a coyote circle a hoop of air in airless space then and now
on the other hand they say that's a good idea you're havin more fun than we us let's all
do it and spin together and chase our tails hey rinkydink hey fire and water

and earth and air hey lallapaloosa magicadabra hey maw look at me
ain't nobody here but us fur-phizzed chickens spinning and spinning
away from the brown/white audience now laughing and laughing
uncontrollably the whole zoo world chasing its tail in a zoo in Yucatan
thinking how silly it is but it is but it ain't but is is but it ain't
dignified like it's quite an idiot phase of the moon supposin somebody notices sees watches
quicklike then stop this crazy cadenza now man stop man wait pause flowerchild
desist like a daisy drooping

Stop
pause to consider the audience raise their noses swish their tails swishily
then maw and paw and the kid yowl and moan and sing hey nonny-na
song more than howl praise more than pain and getting and giving love
from megaphones small as mouths and ears in successive rising and dying sounds
music climbing howling and richocheting off the hunchback clouds back to birthplace sea
—and we the audience laughing like hell and healing our lives
seeing ourselves sometimes single and sometimes joined and pounding our heads like mad

and standing heavily seriously later like a row of drooping cabbage palms in rain
wondering
how many dollars or pieces of eight doubloons and drachmas and pesos it takes
to buy this frightening innocence
again

Yucatan

"I AM SEARCHING FOR YOU"

There are twenty Eskimo words for snow
and many more for different kinds of ice
but two Labrador hunters
in a blue snowmobile failed to recognize
the word for treacherous ice they encountered
when their machine and themselves
drifted away on a floating island
broken from the sea ice
Jacko Onalik and Martin Senigak
you do not know me
have never seen my face
I mean nothing to you
and yet at this moment I am searching
for you 500 feet high
above the fifty or maybe
a hundred kinds of ice below me
and if you are alive down there
might see my eagle shadow
mirrored on the pack ice
might hear dark thunder and look up
Myself clothed in a giant aeroplane
circling in the high clear blue
therefore Martin and Jacko make a sign
I don't know how but make a sign
—and while I'm waiting let me tell you
the odd circumstances of my being here
unmistakable civilian among the uniforms:
six weeks ago I had this bright idea
for writing an article about Search & Rescue
sovereignty overflights and northern patrols
wanted to stare eyeball to eyeball
with Russian trawlers fishing inside
or outside the Canadian twelve-mile limit
carpet-sweeping the ocean of everything alive

So I arranged for that to happen
(made some phone calls to Ottawa)
and here I am with sixteen crewmen
cooking steaks 500 feet above you
in the galley of an Argus aircraft
Anyway at least eight observers up here
are trying to catch sight of the two lost hunters
small black bugs on the white desert
and I am briefly inside the plexiglass bubble
of the aircraft nose feeling like a tear
about to fall back in Nain where village elders
requested the big bird to try one more time
because they are also thinking of you
We have covered 2,000 square miles
of North Atlantic off the Labrador coast today
examining anything the least bit unusual
instruments supplementing the hundred eyes
of Argus in Greek mythology
crossing and re-crossing Dog Island
where you intended to hunt foxes
until the blue snowmobile
misunderstood the word for treacherous ice
as machines sometimes do
leaving a track ending at open water
Jacko Onalik and Martin Senigak
it seems unlikely we shall ever meet
but I wanted you to know something about me
altho I have told you almost nothing
except the fact of searching for you
And now all of us think the search hopeless
the captain and co-pilots and navigators
engineers radio men and observers
and me the civilian
it is hopeless
because six days have come and gone
since you and the blue snowmobile
disappeared in the direction of Dog Island

But I have a reason for writing this
even tho it's absurd to think you could hear
anything said above the high sea barricades
over you and under the aeroplane
—the reason is an illusion
an illusion so strong I feel
I am speaking directly to Jacko and Martin
their souls maybe tho I don't believe in souls
and saying to you we tried all of us tried
because on some night not long delayed
when I have necessity for hope
I hope beforehand someone will be searching
for me however impossible

TROUSERS IN A CLOUD
For Milton Acorn

There was a time or two once when
I figured I could change people
alter their way of thinking
for their own good naturally
I mean even influence the character
of at least a million poems
the sky writes on the sea every morning
Take a case in point take Milton
sleeping on my floor in Montreal
a guy whose non-changing changed me
for an Acorn is at least always an acorn
Genesis began when he woke up
thundered when he wrote a poem
a red rag snatched from the sunset
hammer and sickle tattooed front and rear
like tail lights coming and going
in addition a slow simmering raging calm
blatant dogmatic unchangeable
with a PEI potato for a head
I'd say "Milt for chrissake take a bath"
he'd pay me a gradual half-attention
deciding if what I said was important
or insulting or crazy enough
to break thru his protective fog
as serious say as world revolution
by moonlight among the potato bugs
or the simplicities of good and evil
run riot in Moscow and Washington

But I'm talking as if the guy was dead
nobody this side 1984 has been so alive
he slept and snored on my floor last week
and we still disagree about everything
except this time I keep my mouth shut
about opinions like "We're at war
with the USA"—which is true enough
but I don't wanta be anti-semitic either
(for which I apologize to the Israelis
because that's a lousy comparison)
But re Milt I've never seen a guy
so inarguably right about everything
(except my wife but that's different)
it's like disagreeing with the seasons
a non-imperceptible force of nature
His poems are still like stones
but they have a non-extraordinary smell
that isn't flowers or the mischief
in a man made by women's perfume
for Acorn is earth the crumbling earth
something hunched under rain and wind
phlegmatic as turnips and rutabaga
something that smoulders and endures
falls and rises and stands
In a time when strength is commensurate
(as it always was) with money and power
huge size and million-man armies
Acorn for chrissake—yah I mean him
on some ignored soapbox stands firm
affirms the armour-penetrating truth
highlighting our de-odourized triumphs
and the stink of failure

GATEWAY

As much as any place in the world
I claim this snake fence village
of A-burg as part of myself
its dusty roads and old houses
even the garbage dump sliding
its sleazy treasure chest of litter
and malodourous lastyear valuables
drunkenly down the sudden hill
where winter children toboggan
above two centuries of junk
After the spring run-off in April
at one end of the seasonal time-fuse
before things leap and jump and quiver
and the world explodes with growth
the A-burg kitchen midden is exposed
bright labels faded on tin cans
pop bottles half submerged in dead leaves
broken glass jars from housewives' kitchens
a bulging-bosomed dressmaker's dummy
blurred past its fake human shape
a cracked plow motionless in a black unplowed field
that constitutes the shoreless subterranean world
a wornout catcher's mitt and broken bat
baby carriage shattered past repair
farther down milk churns and old harness
under the earth a rusted flintlock rifle
some horseshoes
maybe a lost green corroded coin
minted in one of the lost Thirteen Colonies
or a Queen Victoria shilling flung here
by a disgusted loser in the non-stop
poker game at the A-burg hotel
even a cracked and useless school blackboard
unstuffed teddy bears and fractured dolls
once even the complete skeleton of a dog

and I suppose there must be other dogs here
farm dogs town dogs sheep dogs lap dogs
dogs that say up yours every time they bark
all kinds of dogs that ever chased chickens
and dug frantically down groundhog holes
all the evil wall-eyed smelly roustabout
pooches mutts curs bitches hounds and mongrels
frenzied pursuers of sheep and rabbits
from Caesar to Genghis Khan and back again
that once were loved by children
here descending the swift/slow elevator of time
reduced to whitening skeletons
All kinds of other bones too
soup bones beef bones pork chop bones
fox bones deer bones wolf bones bear bones
and if I didn't know better
maybe a mammoth's tusk or lizard's forearm
deep down beyond the morning light
that comes bending its way around
this hill a bright flexible shaft of steel
and sees nothing but itself on water
the year's snow or the year's green leaves
or brown land after the spring run-off
the camera eye reversed and turned backwards
showing even myself a man from another time
walking thru the nineteenth-century village
with a kind of jubilation

ACKNOWLEDGEMENTS

CBC Anthology
Canadian Forum
Canadian Literature
Great Canadian Beer Book
Queen's Quarterly
Saturday Night
Jewish Dialog
CrossCountry